Your Healing Journal

SELF-LOVE

The Soul

of A

Queen

Jacke L. Wilson

Author of Planning Your Escape The KEY ...To Your Freedom

Disclaimer: I hold no medical degrees. I am not a doctor, therapist, social worker, or spiritual healer. With that being said, I still believe my knowledge and training as a certified domestic and sexual violence advocate, a Life Recovery Coach coupled with my life experiences can help you to achieve healing and become your authentic unique self. I've discovered a process that has helped me to heal and rebuild my life, after being in an abusive marriage, a few failed relationships, coping with family and childhood issues. I would like to share my healing journey experience with you with hopes this will be encouraging and inspiring to assist you on your healing journey.

GIVE YOURSELF PERMISSION TO HEAL

The ***Love ThySELF Healing Series*** is designed to help encourage and empower women who have endured painful life experiences to reclaim and recover their lives. Are you seeking to gain back control over your emotions? This is guided interactive self-love healing book for you to journal your thoughts, release the painful memories and become a better and stronger version of your ***Authentic Unique Self***.

Life happens to us all in many ways, sometimes we are faced with difficult life experiences such as a relationship ends, loss of a loved one, loss of a job, illness, painful childhood memories, criminal acts, or abuse. During and after the life experiences, we are left to sort out, or in most cases, avoid the emotional remnants that are left. Any one of these unhealed emotions of anger, shame, guilt, rejection, betrayal, fear, pride, and unforgiveness can become an emotional stronghold taking control of your life and leaving you a prisoner of your own thoughts.

This book will act as a map to guide you through discovering your pain points and facing them head on is the pathway to defeat your emotional strongholds on your healing journey to ***Authentic Self-Love***.

Unhealed emotions will become lifetime strongholds, emotions that are healed are liberation for the soul.
- Jacke L. Wilson

From My Heart to Yours

Thank you for purchasing this book, I believe it will help you to heal. This book *"Self-Love Your Healing Journal Book - The Soul of A Queen",* is part of *Love ThySELF Healing Series* and it is the first of its kind. The purpose of this book is to guide you as the reader, on an interactive healing journey, to identify the pain points you are experiencing through the pages of *your* journal entries. This is a great tool to use on your healing journey, if you're a member of a support group, in therapy, considering therapy or working with a life coach. If not, you can use this as a healing tool for yourself or maybe with a loved one to help you identify the root cause of your pain, create a solid foundation to heal, and become FREE from holding onto past hurtful life experiences that have hindered you from living the life you desire.

Inside I will share with you my *Secret Sauce Process* to my healing and how I have been able to maintain it. It's been over eight years and I still practice self-care and self-love every day, I believe practicing self-care and self-love is as vital to us as oxygen is. The suggestions that I share are real life practices that I use consistently to help me stay on a solid foundation throughout my healing journey.

There are three main parts of the secret sauce process that you will need to experience prior to your healing. Facing my emotional strongholds head on, I had to self-evaluate my past relationships and dig deep emotionally to find the true root cause of my pain, which helped me to heal.

Usually, when a person experiences life challenges, often times, they will look at a specific scenario that has happened and their-perception of that situation, justifies the emotions they are feeling as being the root cause of their pain. This is not true because the root cause actually runs deeper inside of you than what you allow people to see on the surface. If we look back over your life challenges, friendships and relationships you will see a pattern or cycle you have

subconsciously been following. You have been attracting the same type of people into your life that keep you surrounded by negative energy.

I greatly appreciate your support with helping me on my mission to help young teenage girls and women become whole, heal past their painful life experiences, discover and walk in their purpose and become their *Authentic Unique Self.*

Note to SELF:

THIS BOOK IS A HEALING JOURNAL. IT WAS NOT WRITTEN TO TRIGGER ANYONE. IF YOU ARE FEELING TRIGGERED WHILE READING AND JOURNALING, PLEASE STOP! TAKE A DEEP BREATH TO CALM YOURSELF DOWN. TAKE A BREAK FROM JOURNALING UNTIL YOU FEEL LIKE YOU ARE IN A BETTER EMOTIONAL STATE, CALL A FRIEND OR SEEK PROFESSIONAL HELP.

Reflections

Dear Queen,

As you began to read and journal your emotions, many memories will begin to surface and your response to the questions may trigger more than one answer to write down. However, in order for this book to be successful with helping you to heal, you will need to dig deeper and look for the root cause of the emotions being displayed in those situations you write down. The root cause is the significate ***painful memories*** you're holding onto, even more so, than the actual situations.

The ***pain points*** (painful memories) that need to be addressed, are only the ones that you feel are holding you back from healing and becoming your Authentic Unique Self. Even though, you may not want to relive some of the life experiences that you have faced, just know that exposing the pain, will help you conquer it and those emotions will no longer control your life, limit your personal growth, hinder you from flourishing in your relationships, your business, or on your job.

Example of digging deep: As a child and many years into adulthood, I hide the fact that I suffered with self-esteem, self-worth and self-confidence issues. Even though, I hid my emotional pain, it still wreaked havoc in my life. Let me show you. The relationships I had in my teen and adult years were unhealthy and not fulfilling because I was unhealthy and so were the guys I dated. I was emotionally broken seeking attention and love from a guy, when I should have been practicing self-love. Had I been practicing this my relationships would have been more fulfilling because I wouldn't have dated those guys that were emotionally unhealthy. Loving myself would have altered my path and life experiences. Reflecting back on your past are you able to relate?

Getting back to what you can expect in this healing journal book. As you read, you will find messages throughout guiding you along and

there are journal pages for you to write down your thoughts based on the topics and questions, and what your mood and energy is like daily. The quotes will help you to stay encouraged and inspired to stay the course on your healing journey.

It is my hope that this book, ***"Self-Love Your Healing Journal Book",*** is successful with helping you to release those painful memories so you can heal. Becoming your Authentic Unique Self will help you to have more fulfilling relationships with your friends and the people you love.

Note to SELF:

It's time to take back control of your emotions and your life so that you can be FREE of emotional strongholds and live the life you desire!

Introduction: My Backstory

In the beginning of my healing journey, I discovered, the emotions that I was holding onto as an adult, some of the pain was from my childhood and the rest was from my adult life experiences. These experiences had negatively formed my perception of life, relationships, love and of myself. As a result, I struggled with low self-esteem, low self-worth, no confidence and not truly loving myself.

For many years, throughout my adult life, I hide that fact and I pretended to be whole. Isn't that what we are supposed to do? Act strong when we really want to cry. We wear the facade that everything in our life is great and we have it going on? Pretending to be happy when we are sad or emotionally bankrupt. When all the while, we are wearing different masks throughout various stages of our life and the little girl inside of us is screaming for help. Screaming to be heard. Screaming to be understood, Screaming to be accepted. Screaming to be respected. Screaming to be LOVED. Her unanswered screams are a sign of her emotional detachment, which becomes a gateway to attracting emotionally unavailable mates. Remember -like attracts like.

Back to my story, years later, I dated and married a man I believed to be my soul mate. I had no idea that I would suffer years of emotional, psychological, spiritual, and financial abuse at the hands of someone that said he loved me many times.

Fast-forward to today, I made it through those difficult times to come out on the other side stronger, confident, in love with myself, and happier than I have ever been in my life. Reading through the pages and journaling, you will gain insight into my **Secret Sauce Process** on how I was able to go from an angry, unhealed, and unforgiving woman to a loving, healed, and forgiving woman. My transition happened for a couple of reasons. First, I wanted to be free from depression and let go of holding onto the painful memories, and hurtful emotions every time I thought about my failed marriage and the abuse. Second, it was important for me to take back control of my life and stop letting my emotions control me.

I want the same for you to be …FREE. I wish you much success using this, **"Self-Love: Your Healing Journal Book."** It is my hope that by the end of this book you will have gained knowledge and understanding of the importance of **Authentic Self-Love** and becoming your **Authentic Unique Self.** I wish you much success accomplishing your healing goals and creating a more fulfilling lifestyle. Happy reading!

Note to SELF:

Denying yourself your rightful place of being healed, will not create a happy and fulfilling life for you. Unhealed painful memories will affect your mind, body, and soul with stress, depression, and unhappiness.

{ We all have a story to tell to help someone. Please share your story, this will help you to heal. }

Praise Moments

I AM SO PROUD OF YOU! Thank you for sharing your story. This is a huge step in the right direction to build a solid foundation on your healing journey. You are very brave and when you decide to share your story with others or maybe even write a book about your story, your life will be encouragement to some, inspiration to others and empowerment to many.

Note to SELF:

Unhealed emotions will become lifetime strongholds, emotions that are healed are liberation for the soul.
- *Jacke L. Wilson*

Diving Deep

We have touched on a lot of material so far which has really laid down the foundation of what this book, ***"Self-Love: The Soul of A Queen - Your Healing Journal Book"***, is really about. The mission of this book is to be an interactive guide, so feel free to write in the book because this is your healing journal. By reading this book and answering the questions, gives you, as the reader, the opportunity to dig deep into your soul. You will also discover what the root cause of your pain is which will allow you to heal from your painful memories.

I believe in you! It is my desire that by the end of this book your self-esteem, self-worth, and confidence will increase regarding your ability to heal from your past. You got this!

{ Self-check. Please write down what your mood is like and how you are feeling before you start journaling. }

From My Heart to Yours

Dear Queen,

Thank you for sharing how you are feeling; I know this isn't easy to do. Being vulnerable, sharing your deep emotions, and feelings about your painful experiences opens old wounds and may trigger painful memories. When you are triggered by something from your past and the memories take you back to that exact day or time and you feel the same emotions that you felt back then, this is an area that needs your attention because you have not healed from this experience. Your mind and body is still reacting to that situation as if it is happening again in your current life because you are still emotionally connected to it. In order to eliminate that from continuing to happen, you have to disconnect yourself emotionally from that life experience. If not, this experience will continue to control you emotionally and hinder you from living a fulfilling and happy life

At any point in this book if you start to feel any anxiety or stress, please stop and take a break away from the book, until you are not experiencing those emotions. Seek help from a friend or seek professional help. If your anxiety and depression increase while journaling in this book, I would suggest that you stop and seek professional help. You may not be ready to face your pain at this time by yourself; but if you decide to continue my suggestion would be to incorporate this healing journal in with your sessions to help you along your healing journey.

Please remember, this is a self-guided healing journal so there is no deadline to finish this book, please go at your own pace.

Vulnerability is the birthplace of innovation, creativity, and change.
— *Brene' Brown*

Are you ready?

Dear Queen,

This process will not be a walk in the park but it will help you to acknowledge you have pain points, one by one face them so that you can be healed, live a more fulfilling life, and become your Authentic Unique Self.

One suggestion that I have for you is to make a promise to yourself that you are going to stay committed on your healing journey. This part is very important because we make promises to others and we put forth necessary effort to keep that promise. However, when it comes to ourselves, we often fall short. I would like for you to promise yourself that you will stay committed to seeking help with your healing and this book, "Self-Love Your Healing Journal Book," is your first step with creating a solid foundation to heal. Repeat the previous sentence a couple of times. Make it personal so it will connect deep in your mind and heart.

If you are in group session or therapy, please let them know that you are using this book as a form of therapy to heal. Incorporating this book with your sessions, is a great way to express your emotional strongholds and share with your therapist while he/she helps you on your healing journey. If you are not in therapy, this book is a great way to identify through your journaling the emotions that are hindering you from healing. Feel free to buddy with a friend as you read this book for moral support.

If you are truly honest with yourself about the emotions you are currently feeling or have been holding onto, this book is intended to act as a healing guide to help you understand and map out why you are stuck in certain areas of your life. As humans, we are faced with different life experiences. Some of these memories we are able to let go of and move forward knowing and believing that these experiences we had, served as an opportunity for personal growth. On the other hand, there are some life experiences that we faced, where the painful experiences and memories penetrated our heart, mind, and soul to the point where letting go and moving on, seems *very* impossible.

On the following pages, you will find questions that will challenge to remember certain times in your life where you experienced a pain point. There may be more than one time you felt or experienced that emotion, however, the experience that you believe is still weighing heavy on you today is the one that you should write down. Your perception of these situations and emotional strongholds that are controlling your life as you journal your thoughts in this book you will find out why.

As you read through the pages of the book, if there is a topic within one of the weeks that does not pertain to you, then write down an emotion that does and continue to answer the questions.

It's time to let go of your emotional strongholds and establish a solid foundation to let healing begin. You deserve for your life to be happier and more fulfilling. Happiness is formed and nurtured on the inside of you. No one else is in charge of your happiness, only you.

Note to SELF:

The most rewarding relationship you will ever
have, is the one you have with yourself.
Jacke L. Wilson

WEEK 1

Anger

Let's Chat

This week we're going to chat about **anger**. On the following pages, write down what you are thinking and how you are feeling about expressing your emotions about **anger**.

Note to SELF:

If you don't release the feelings of anger you have and forgive that person that pain will become a lifetime emotional stronghold.

What is Anger

Kim Pratt, LCSW. February 3, 2014, accessed 28 May 2020, Healthy Tools: What is Anger? A secondary Emotion, www.healthypsych.com/psychology-tools-what-is-anger-a-secondary-emotion

According to *Psychology Today*, feeling anger is a natural part of being human and it is an internal alarm that tells us something is not quite right.

What many people don't realize is that anger is a secondary emotion. Typically, one of the primary emotions, like fear or sadness, can be found underneath the anger. Fear includes things like anxiety and worry, and sadness comes from the experience of loss, disappointment or discouragement.

This is a good read article. See link above.

Reflections

Dear Queen,

Understanding that anger is a second emotion, what thoughts ran through your head? When I first heard this reasoning, I was like there is no way this could be true. Remembering a painful life experience, I was reminded that there was another emotion I felt before the anger kicked in. After doing an emotional deep dive, I realized that statement was very true.

When we encounter life experiences, most times, we tend to only look at the surface of that situation. We look at what happened, who caused it and why we believe it happened. If we look deeper into the situation/s, we might find there are certain patterns that recycled or patterns of limited beliefs about the situation/s.

If you or someone you know has endured a tragedy like abuse or sexual assault as a child or an adult, we know that tragedy was NOT yours or their fault. The perpetrator is FULLY responsible for inflicting pain on you or them. As a result of this happening you may be left with anger towards that person, rightfully so, or you may project those feelings of anger towards yourself because you weren't able to protect yourself from that person. Feeling anger towards yourself for someone else's negative behaviors towards you, creates a place inside of you for negative energy to flow igniting an atmosphere for you to practice "self-abuse" instead of "self-love."

Practicing self-love is foreign to many people, including **myself,** because I wasn't taught to practice this. I was taught to be strong and deal with whatever life challenges came my way. I was taught to push through it and have a do what you have to do kind of attitude. This way of thinking did not come with instructions on how to do it. I watched older family members and mirrored what they did, even though they weren't given instructions either. So the moral is, no one really knew what to do. These were limited beliefs lacking answers or solutions that were passed down from previous generations.

It's important to know who you are and practice self-love. This will help you discover your **Authentic Unique Self**.

Note to SELF:

Where there is anger, there is always pain underneath.
- Eckhart Tolle

{ You are beautiful and intelligent. Repeat this daily. }

Date _____

Today's Energy? Low - Medium - High _____

Today's Mood _____

Release the Chatter: Write about your energy and mood for today.

_____
_____
_____
_____
_____
_____
_____
_____
_____
_____
_____
_____
_____
_____
_____
_____
_____
_____
_____
_____
_____
_____

{ Take a moment to reflect on your thoughts. Have you ever experienced anger? At what age? Please share. }

{ Is there something you believe that you could have done differently to prevent experiencing anger? }

{ Were you able to overcome the feelings of anger? If yes how? If no, what is keeping you from letting go? }

{ What actions have you taken to rebuild your self-esteem after the impact from anger? }

Keeping it Real

When you love a person, it is not easy to turn off your emotions when they do or say something that is hurtful. It takes time to unlove a person. Don't rush the process, acknowledge and own your emotions, be it positive or negative, so you can heal.

WEEK 2

Shame

Let's Chat

This week we are going to chat about **shame**. On the following pages write down what you are thinking and how you are feeling about expressing your feelings/emotions about **shame**.

Note to SELF:

If you don't forgive yourself for the shame you experienced this will become a lifetime emotional stronghold.

What is Shame

Shame is an emotion that individuals feel on a personal bases regarding their own life. It is our internal thoughts, and this is where our self-worth is challenged and determines our self-esteem level. Shame is more of an internal feeling of how one compares their life to someone else's. Shame can also be how one perceives their self-image. When a person feels shame it is more closely related to how their self-esteem or status in life is. An individual can feel shame or embarrassment because they don't have the basic necessities to maintain daily living. A person can feel shame regarding their career status and finances.

Shame is like a wound that is never exposed and therefore never heals.
 -Andreas Eschbach

> Grace means that all of your mistakes now serve a purpose instead of serving shame.
> *- Brene' Brown*

Date _____

Today's Energy? Low - Medium - High _____

Today's Mood _____

Release the Chatter: Write about your energy and mood for today.

_____
_____
_____
_____
_____
_____
_____
_____
_____
_____
_____
_____
_____
_____
_____
_____
_____
_____
_____
_____
_____
_____

{ Take a moment to reflect on your thoughts. Can you name a time when you felt shame? At what age? }

{ Is there something you believe you could have done differently to prevent experiencing shame. }

{ Were you able to overcome the feelings of shame? If yes, how? If no, what is keeping you from letting go? }

{ What actions did you take to work on rebuilding your self-esteem to overcome feelings of shame? }

{ What is your energy and mood like after writing down your thoughts about shame? }

Reflections

Dear Queen,

Reflect on your emotions for the rest of this week or if you need more time before going onto the next week's topic. Day-by-day focus on ways to build your self-esteem up and decrease the negative emotions and actions that shame has had on your life.

Here are a few suggestions of activities that you can practice during the weeks before you move onto the next week. This is also a good practice to help you on your journey after you have completed your journal entries. Practicing this everyday will help you with creating **Authentic Self-Love** and becoming your **Authentic Unique Self.**

- Create post-it notes on your mirror or high traffic places in your home/apartment, etc., with positive words of affirmations to help build up your self-esteem and self-worth.
- Take a pic of yourself and post it up in your room or keep it in this book to remind you that you are a beautiful and intelligent woman.
- These practices will help strengthen your commitment to stay on your healing journey.

Note to SELF:

See yourself through your lens not through the lens
of your past or other people
- Jacke L. Wilson

WEEK 3

Guilt

Let's Chat

This week we are going to chat about *guilt*. On the following pages write down what you are thinking and how you are feeling about expressing your thoughts about a time you experienced *guilt*.

Note to SELF:

If feeling guilty about something you did or said is not forgiven it will weight on you and become a lifetime emotional stronghold.

What is Guilt

Guilt is an emotion we feel when we do or say something wrong. Guilt is an admission to doing or saying something wrong. It relates more to a moral standpoint, such as what is right and wrong. Guilt is more about a person's beliefs regarding what is moral and immoral in any situation. It is a feeling that we feel when we take responsibility for actions or behaviors that we regret. We feel guilt when we own up to our actions whether good or bad. There are other emotions that a person feels when they accept responsibility for their actions or behaviors, such as feeling unworthy, or embarrassed. Guilt can also work in a positive way. It works from a moral standpoint it can also help guide people into living a life maintaining standards of doing what is right and not what is right.

You have permission to walk away, without carrying any guilt.
 - Maryam Hasnaa

{ No amount of guilt can change the past and no amount of worrying can change the future. }
- Unknown

Date _____

Today's Energy? Low - Medium - High _____

Today's Mood _____

Release the Chatter: Write about your energy and mood for today.

_____
_____
_____
_____
_____
_____
_____
_____
_____
_____
_____
_____
_____
_____
_____
_____
_____
_____

{ Take a moment to reflect on your thoughts. Have you ever experienced guilt? At what age? Please share. }

{ Is there something you believe you could have done differently to prevent experiencing guilt? }

{ Were you able to overcome the feelings of guilt? If yes, how? If no, what is keeping you from letting go? }

{ Please share what your energy and mood is after writing down your thoughts about feeling guilty? }

{ What actions have you taken to rebuild your self-esteem and overcome guilt? }

Reflections

Dear Queen,

Let me share this with you. Holding onto any emotional guilt is not healthy. Sometimes we are holding onto emotional guilt that isn't ours to carry but because we blamed ourselves in that situation, we take on the emotional guilt. We carry a burden that we shouldn't be carrying.

If we played a part in that situation that caused guilt then yes, we must be held accountable for the emotional guilt that we caused. With that being said, we should not hold onto the guilt for dear life. We still need to heal from the emotional guilt so that it will not become a lifetime stronghold.

There is this unwritten rule that has been etched in the mindset of many people I have coached, including myself, to believe, if you leave from the situation you no longer are present or emotionally connected to the chaos. This mindset has been their perception of removing yourself physically from the situation as their form of healing. For a number of years this was my understanding. This is so far from the truth and is a false sense of healing to believe that just because you leave the situation you are healed.

Healing affects every area of our lives. Healing starts from within and will shine on the outside of the person's life through their character, their faith, the interactions they have with others, the healthy relationships they have, and their personal and professional success.

I have been guilty of holding onto emotional guilt. I held onto the failure of my marriage. Even though my ex had an affair he blamed me for his reasons for cheating. I held onto the blame and guilt when it wasn't mine to carry.

Please, let go of the guilt!

{ You have made it to three weeks so far with journaling your thoughts. YAY! How are you feeling? }

Praise Moments

Congratulations!! You have made it to week three on your journey to heal from your past life experiences. YAY! You are continuing to make the best decision you could make by choosing you and your well-being first. You deserve to be happy. It's okay to smile.

Note to SELF:

It's time to take back control of your emotions and your life so that you can be FREE of emotional strongholds and live the life you desire!

WEEK 4

Rejection

What is Rejection

Merriam Webster Dictionary says this about rejection; Rejection is the action of rejecting: the state of being rejected

https://www.merriam-webster.com/dictionary/rejection

Hanna Rose LCPC, *Posted June 23, 2019* – Facing Rejection, It isn't easy, it's seldom graceful, but it is doable, *accessed May .25, 2020,* <https://www.psychologytoday.com/us/blog/working-through-shame/201906/facing-rejection>

Facing Rejection

It isn't easy, it's seldom graceful, but it is doable

The lessons of rejection can be delivered in a myriad of forms: a relationship ending, a school denying your application, a job opportunity that was given to someone else, a conversation that ends abruptly, an omission of a compliment, a lack of emotional availability, and so many more.

But the common thread that seems to permeate through every experience of rejection is almost impossible to ignore: the deterioration of self-worth.

That is the most dangerous part about the experience of rejection. We internalize it. We make it about us. We tell ourselves these narratives about how we aren't good enough, how we aren't worthy. But that's simply not true. We are always worthy; we are always enough. Maybe the relationship itself wasn't organic, maybe it's not meeting both of your needs. But that doesn't mean you are inherently flawed.

Let's Chat

This week we are going to chat about *rejection*. On the next couple of pages write down what you are thinking and how you are feeling about expressing your feelings/emotions about *rejection*.

Note to SELF:

You are enough. You are the right height. You are the right size. You have the right skin color... Love your Authentic Unique Self. You are enough.
- Jacke L. Wilson

Reflections

Dear Queen,

At some point in our lives we all have experienced rejection. How we handle are emotions and feelings will dictate the outcome. If we learn to accept the rejections we face as a learning experience and not take it personally, we will have less stress and emotionally we will recover quicker. When we hold onto rejection our emotions, and feelings, create negative energy. This negative energy will flow through us for days, months, and years contributing to low self-esteem, low self-worth, and lack of confidence.

During this week, you will be asked to write down your experience with rejection. Write down the experience that really impacted your life, it might be an event that happened some time ago but is still impacting your life today. Let's talk about this experience so that you can let go of these negative emotions and continue with your healing process.

READY, SET, GO!

Note to Self:

Remember someone else's negative opinions of you are unsolicited
- *Jacke L. Wilson*

*Every time I thought I was being rejected from something good,
I was actually being re-directed to something better.*
- Dr. Steve Maraboli

> { What feels like rejection is often God's protection
> when you're heading in the wrong direction.
> - Donna Partow }

Date _____

Today's Energy? Low - Medium - High _____

Today's Mood _____

Release the Chatter: Write about your energy and mood for today.

{ Take a moment to reflect on your thoughts. Can you name a time when you felt rejection? Please share. }

{ Is there something you believe you could have done different to prevent experiencing rejection? }

{ Were you able to overcome the feelings of rejection?
If yes, how? If no, why haven't you let go? }

{ What actions have you taken to work on rebuilding your self-esteem to overcome feelings of rejection? }

{ Please share what your energy and mood is after sharing your thoughts on rejection. }

Keeping it Real

No one likes to feel rejection. We often take the rejection personal. I remember the day I felt rejection when I found out my husband at the time, stepped out of our marriage and had an affair with a lady from the same church we attended. This was very embarrassing. I was devasted. I felt helpless and hopeless not knowing what to do to try and fix our broken marriage or how to persuade him to end the affair.

Releasing myself from hurt emotions was very difficult to do because I somehow felt like it was my fault, even though I know that he made the conscious decision to step out of our marriage. Eventually, I forgave myself for holding onto rejection and feelings of guilt then I was able to heal. Also, my faith is God helped me to heal and move on.

Sometimes we believe we are being rejected from a person or situation, often times, we're simply being redirected from an unhealthy situation or from a toxic person. Look at rejection as another way of saying the famous quote, "you dodged that bullet.

Note to SELF:

Don't personalize rejection. Often times the flaw is in the other person.
- Dr. Phil

WEEK 5

Betrayal

What is Betrayal?

According to Webster, betrayal is the act of betraying someone or something or the fact of being betrayed: violation of a person's trust or confidence, of a moral standard, the revelation of something hidden or secret.

Let's Chat

This week we are going to chat about ***betrayal***. On the next couple of pages write down what you are thinking and how you are feeling about expressing your feelings/emotions about ***betrayal***.

Note to SELF:

If the emotions you are holding onto from being betrayed are not forgiven, they will become a lifetime emotional stronghold.

Betrayal leaves us at a fork in the road… we can become struck in a bad moment forever or we can put it behind us for good. We decide our path
 - *Carmen Harra*

> When someone betrays you, it is a reflection
> of their character, not yours.
> *- Unknown*

Date _____

Today's Energy? Low - Medium - High _____

Today's Mood _____

Release the Chatter: Write about your energy and mood for today.

_____

_____

_____

_____

_____

_____

_____

_____

_____

_____

_____

_____

_____

_____

_____

_____

_____

_____

_____

{ Take a moment to reflect on your thoughts. Have you ever experienced betrayal? Please share. }

{ Is there something you could have done different to prevent experiencing betrayal? }

{ Were you able to overcome the feelings of betrayal? If yes, how? If no, what is keeping you from letting go? }

{ What actions have you taken to work on rebuilding your self-esteem and overcome feelings of betrayal? }

{ Please share what your energy and mood is after sharing your thoughts on betrayal. }

Reflections

Dear Queen,

Betrayal enters our lives wearing many disguises. Some we are able to detect and others we aren't. The ones we can't detect are the ones that sneak up on us and catch us off guard. We are floored when these betrayals are discovered. We are devasted by the betrayal and wonder if there were signs and how did we miss them. The pain of it all runs so deep within our heart, mind, and soul taking us to the front door of blame. We begin to judge our character and question the type of person we are. How could I have not known? Am I stupid? Am I not intelligent enough to have seen this coming? Am I that weak that I overlooked all the signs? I thought I was a good judge of character. Was the love I have for this person 'not enough? Was I not enough? Do I know how to love? Maybe I don't know how to love, and this is why I've been betrayed. This has happened before; it's not meant for me to be happy in love. Relationships are overrated. This marriage didn't work, I'm done.

Did you notice how one doubtful question turned into a series of doubtful questions eventually turning into blame, guilt, and self-defeating thoughts? Not one of the questions asked was positive. Not one of the questions put the blame on the guilty party which is the only one guilty of betrayal.

In my personal experience and years of helping others on their healing journey, blaming ourselves is like second nature. We're on autopilot, we do it without even thinking about it. This type of behavior is not healthy and will prolong healing.

WEEK 6

Fear

What is Fear

According to *Merriam Webster Dictionary*, fear is an unpleasant often strong emotion caused by anticipation or awareness of danger.

Note to SELF:

Sometime fear can have a positive outcome. What I mean is you purchased or someone else purchased this book for you to help you sort out your painful memories. I am sure in the beginning this seemed pretty scary for you to journal your thoughts in this book but guess what the outcome will be healing. So, we don't always have to fear fear, it can be a good thing.

Let's Chat

This week we are going to chat about *fear*. On the following pages write down what you are thinking and how you are feeling about expressing your feelings/emotions about *fear*.

Note to SELF:

If you're holding onto feelings of fear towards someone, you are giving them control over your life and this will become an emotional lifetime stronghold.

> Fear can only grow in darkness once you
> face fear with light, you win
> - Dr. *Steve Maraboli*

Date _____

Today's Energy? Low - Medium - High _____

Today's Mood _____

Release the Chatter: Write about your energy and mood for today.

_____
_____
_____
_____
_____
_____
_____
_____
_____
_____
_____
_____
_____
_____
_____

{ Take a moment to reflect on your thoughts. Have you ever experienced fear? At what age? Please share. }

{ Is there something you believe you could have done differently to prevent experiencing fear? }

{ Were you able to overcome the feelings of fear? If yes, how? If no, what is keeping you from letting go? }

{ What actions have you taken to work on rebuilding your self-esteem to overcome your feelings of fear? }

{ Please share what your energy and mood is after writing down your thoughts about fear. }

Reflections

Dear Queen,

We all have faced some life challenges that have caused us to feel fear. I heard fear explained as **FEAR is False Evidence Appearing Real.** When the fearful situation is happening, it does not feel at all like it is false evidence appearing real, at that moment it is very real. I believe this sounds better **FEAR is Factual Evidence Appearing Real.**

Even if you are experiencing a life challenge that is fearful there is still help available for you. You must take the first step to reach out for help. There are many crisis helplines available to chat with you and help you sort things out.

I experienced fear prior to my divorce when I knew I had to start my life over as a single mom with two daughters, one in college and the other in middle school. How was I going to manage this new life? Fear overwhelmed me and I spent many nights crying, blaming myself, and feeling like a failure. My faith in God helped me to overcome those feelings and to eventually get my life back on track.

Note to SELF:

Feel the fear and do it anyway.
Dr. Susan Jeffers

WEEK 7

Pride

Let's Chat

This week we are going to chat about ***pride***. On the next couple of pages write down what you are thinking and how you are feeling about expressing your feelings/emotions about ***pride***.

Note to SELF:

If you are holding onto the feelings of not being able to forgive the person that hurt, you unforgiveness will become a lifetime of emotional stronghold.

Pride is concerned with who is right, humility is concerned with what is right.
- Ezra T. Benson

> Take pride in how far you've come and
> have faith in how far you can go.
> - *Paula Finn*

Date _____

Today's Energy? Low - Medium - High _____

Today's Mood _____

Release the Chatter: Write about your energy and mood for today.

_____
_____
_____
_____
_____
_____
_____
_____
_____
_____
_____
_____
_____
_____
_____
_____
_____
_____
_____
_____

{ Take a moment to reflect on your thoughts. Have you ever experienced feelings of pride? At what age? }

{ Is there something you believe that you could have done different in the way that you exhibited pride? }

{ What actions have you taken to free yourself of prideful thoughts or behavior? }

{ Please share what your energy and mood is after sharing your thoughts about being prideful. }

Reflections

Dear Queen,

It's okay to be proud of the accomplishments that you achieved and your personal wins, just don't become full of yourself and forget on occasions to eat a slice of humbled pie. Humility will win every time and generally people like to be around others that are humbled, fun and interesting not around people that are cocky, condescending and not fun.

When I think about pride the only thought comes to mine is a scripture that I remember reading as a teenager. "Pride goes before destruction, a haughty spirit before a fall." Proverbs 16:18 NIV. As a teen I remember saying I never want to be this type of person. Even to this day I can still say that I never want to be this person.

Do we really know if we are or have been a prideful person? Chances are we have at some point in our life. Maybe we were able to check ourselves when we realized we were walking in pride or maybe we weren't. If we're eating humbled pie often this is a way to keep ourselves in check. Also, if we surround ourselves with positive and caring people that are upfront enough to tell us when we are acting out of pride, humility will be our personal guide.

Note to SELF:

You can't make decisions based on fear and the possibility of what might happen.
- *Michelle Obama*

WEEK 8

Forgiveness

What is Forgiveness

According to *Cambridge Dictionary*, forgiveness, to stop blaming or being angry with someone for something that person has done or not punish them for something.

Fred Luskins, "n.d.". Greater Good Magazine - Science-Based Insights for A Meaningful Life, What is Forgiveness, <https://greatergood.berkeley.edu/topic/forgiveness/definition#what-is-forgiveness>

What is Forgiveness?

Psychologist generally define forgiveness as a conscious, deliberate decision to release feelings of resentment or vengeance toward a person or group who has harmed you, regardless of whether they actually deserve your forgiveness.

Just as important as defining what forgiveness is, though, is understanding what forgiveness is *not*. Experts who study or teach forgiveness make clear that when you forgive, you do not gloss over or deny the seriousness of an offense against you. Forgiveness does not mean forgetting, not does it mean condoning or excusing offenses. Though forgiveness can help repair a damaged relationship, it doesn't obligate you to reconcile with the person who harmed you or release them from legal accountability.

Instead, forgiveness brings the forgiver peace of mind and frees him or her from corrosive anger. While there is some debate over whether true forgiveness requires positive feelings toward the offender, experts agree that it at least involves letting go of deeply held negative feelings. In that way, it empowers you to heal and move on with your life.

Let's Chat

This week we are going to chat about *forgiveness*. On the following pages write down what you are thinking and how you are feeling about expressing your thoughts about *forgiveness*?

Note to SELF:

If unforgiveness is not forgiven it becomes a lifetime emotional stronghold. You lose your control over your emotions when you hold onto unforgiveness.

Forgiveness provides hope, joy, and a bright future that nothing else can.
  - *Paul J Meyer*

> Hating someone and holding onto bitterness
> builds a prison around us
> -Steve Saint

Date _____

Today's Energy? Low - Medium - High _____

Today's Mood _____

Release the Chatter: Write about your energy and mood for today.

_____
_____
_____
_____
_____
_____
_____
_____
_____
_____
_____
_____
_____
_____
_____
_____
_____
_____

{ Have you ever forgave someone for doing or saying something hurtful to you? Please share. }

{ How did you feel after you forgave that person? }

{ Have you ever wanted someone to forgive you for something you did or said to them? Please share. }

{ Why is it important to you to receive forgiveness from this person? Please share. }

{ After you read the article about what forgiveness is has your mindset changed? Please share. }

{ Share a time in your life when you were happy. }

{ What does happiness mean to you? }

{ Have you experienced victory in any area of your life when you felt emotionally bound? }

Reflections

Dear Queen,

Our self-esteem, self-worth and the level of love we have for ourselves is also connected to the emotional strongholds we carry through life. Take responsibility for your actions, forgive yourself, and forgive others for the part they played in your life experience so that you can move on. You will have freedom and no longer feel pain, guilt, and unforgiveness. There is a bright future ahead of you with many opportunities to pursue. Once you complete your healing journey you will be able to fulfill your life purpose.

A great book to read about forgiveness is
Forgiveness …the Ultimate Miracle by Paul J. Meyer

I read this book and I gained so much knowledge and understanding about what forgiveness is not, what forgiveness is, and how important forgiveness is to the person that has been hurt. Forgiveness is not about giving the person that hurt you a pass. When you forgive a person for the pain, they caused you, you take back control and you release the negative energy you carried inside.

If we have hurt someone, it's natural to want them to forgive you. Sometimes they will and sometimes they won't. I learned from the book above, even if the person doesn't forgive you, you have to be able to accept and respect their decision. You asked for forgiveness from them and they refused, now you have to release yourself from that negative energy by forgiving yourself because you hurt them. When you forgive yourself, it is time to move on no longer with guilt or shame.

Forgiveness is freedom to the one who chooses to forgive.

{ Write down as many positive words to describe who you are to a new friend. }

{ Write down some hobbies, interest, or talents that you have. }

Discovery time

Dear Queen,

You have journaled your thoughts and experiences, have you found similarities in any of your life experiences? Are the same emotions appearing in the different life challenges that you have shared? Have you found any patterns of beliefs that are in each experience? Are these experiences with the same person or a different person? Have you figured out which emotion/s you have difficulty letting go?

These questions that I am asking you are found within your journal entries and in the life situations that you have experienced but haven't spoken or written about them but they have made a home in your mind and in your heart. When we are hurt by someone, we carry those hurtful memories for a very long time. There are some people that have not healed from the pain they experienced as a child and they are adults now, still holding onto those painful memories.

It is my hope that you have identified your pain points but if you haven't yet, let's keep going to the next part which we will discuss about wearing masks. I believe this will help to make things crystal clear.

Let's chat about the different mask/s people wear to hide the hurt and pain they are experiencing. As you read over the brief descriptions of each mask think about which one applies to you. You may notice that you relate to more than one and that is very possible. The mask you wear often; you will relate to the description that describes your behaviors the most. Discovering which mask, you're wearing will help you to better identify and understand, your thoughts about yourself, your behaviors and responses when interacting with other people and how you cope with life challenges.

Remove The Mask

What is the meaning behind these sayings, "Remove The Mask" or "Take off That Mask?" According to *Psych Central,* we wear different kinds of masks to keep ourselves from getting hurt. (psychcentral.com). See below the 10 different masks.

The 10 Masks We Wear

1. The Cool Guy

By all outward appearances, this person seems to have mastered whatever it takes to stay calm in all situations. Unrattled by conflict or chaos, this person possesses the composure of a Tibetan Monk. However, beneath the surface, one of two things happen. His bottled-up emotions either result in a nervous breakdown, or he periodically presses the release valve when no one is around, snapping at folks.

2. The Humorist

Humor is a brilliant defense mechanism. If you're laughing, you're not crying, even though they look the same. Sarcasm, especially, tends to be rooted in pain and is not without consequence. Uncomfortable with conflict, he will charm his way out of confrontation. His comedy serves as a protective shield. As such, he doesn't allow anyone in, and is lonely.

3. The Overachiever

Some people unconsciously pursue perfectionism as a defense against annihilation. If everything is done right, then their world can't fall apart. While the accolades and praises associated with being a perfectionist may provide some temporary relief, the perfectionist is always at the mercy of something going wrong, and therefore live in a constant state of anxiety. Her stubbornness, obsessiveness, and lack of trust build a barrier between her and her loved ones.

4. The Martyr

Most of us know a martyr, a person who boasts that she has single-handedly saved the world with her selfless actions. While martyrs can bring families together with compassion, their exaggeration of sacrifices drives loved ones away. The drama with which they do good serves as a protective shield from the very people who they are helping. The martyr secures her place in the world by believing her role is critical, all the while making everyone uncomfortable around her.

5. The Bully

Their assertion of control can be subtle, a gentle manipulation to make you see it their way, or can be aggressive, even physical. While bullies appear to be confident in their forceful delivery of opinions and order, they are innately insecure. They want so badly to be respected that they will break the rules of appropriate conduct to get that esteem. Self-doubt drives their hostile behavior; an obsessive need to feel right that comes at the expense of others' rights and feelings

6. The Control Freak

The control freak uses order and power to achieve a sense of security. By making sure everything is in its proper place, he relieves his fear of the unknown, of ambiguity, or uncertainty. A mother hen, the control freak won't let anyone out of her sight, and assumes responsibility for all those around her, even when they don't want to be cared for. He becomes unraveled when anyone deviates from the plan.

7. The Self-Basher

Suffering from a chronic case of unworthiness and insecurity, the self-basher projects a negative view of herself to others. Perhaps unconsciously, she believes that she can insulate herself from hurt by hurting herself first. She, then, berates herself and insults herself as a protective measure against any potential zinger coming her way.

Self-deprecation becomes a defense mechanism with which she avoids any risk of intimacy

8. The People-Pleaser

The people-pleasure will go to desperate lengths to win the approval of those around her, because her sense of identity is largely based on the assessment of others. Her values often vacillate depending on the input of the day because she looks to outside sources to validate who she is. This mask-type solicits the advice of friends, doctors, experts, co-workers, and mentors because she lacks strong foundation. Easily influenced by others, decisions are difficult for her.

9. The Introvert

The timid person or introvert is deathly afraid of failure and rejection. He would much rather feel the pangs of loneliness than risk not being liked. Like the perfectionist, he is so afraid of making a mistake that he refuses to challenge himself. He blushes easily, is embarrassed easily, and doesn't say much for fear of saying the wrong thing.

10. The Social Butterfly

Although the life of the party, the social butterfly is innately lonely. He compensates for feelings of insecurity with his gift of gab and small talk. He has many acquaintances but few, if any, real friends. Although his calendar is packed full of social events, his life lacks meaning. He keeps his conversations superficial because deeper dialogues may expose his anxiety or shed his confident persona.

*This part is very important; on the following pages you will have a chance to write down which mask/s you relate to. You will also have space to explain your reasons why you believe you are or have been wearing that particular mask. Be honest as you give your reasons because this is also a part of releasing your pain so you can heal, love yourself, and become your **Authentic Unique Self**.

{ Which mask did you identify with? Why? Please share your thoughts. }

Reflections

Dear Queen,

Self-love is vital to your well-being. If you don't learn to truly love yourself and all of your flaws, you will be guided by the opinions of others and seeking their approval will be more important to you than making your own decisions.

Hopefully by now you have identified your pain points and the mask/s you have worn throughout the years of deflecting your pain. Have you noticed a specific pattern that has been a part of each life challenge? The patterns that you have found has it helped you to understand how or why you faced these life challenges? Has it helped you to understand why you keep attracting the same type of people in your life?

Reflecting back to the different masks, you may relate with more than one of the masks, no problem. If you relate more with the people pleaser mask that would make sense because we as woman are more of the nurturing type of people and most times, we sacrifice our time, money, and sleep to help out a loved one. We are very quick to jump into action when a crisis happens even if the crisis is someone else's we still look for some form of resolution. Because we are like this, we definitely need to have boundaries in place.

Once you establish boundaries, you will learn more about the people in your life. With some of them nothing will change they will respect your boundaries and continue to be your friend or business associate, however the other ones will not like the boundaries and will push back on them often. When we find that the people in our lives are not respecting our boundaries, its' time to reevaluate our boundaries to see if they need to be changed because they are not giving us the protection we need or if it's our fault because we have not been enforcing them. Let's be honest. Majority of the time it's our fault.

Let me share this with you. Back in my time, the older generations didn't educate the us on the importance of self-love, we were taught to be of service to others. If you spoke too highly of yourself then you were considered to be vain or conceited. How were we supposed to learn how to love ourselves? The idea of it was hardly mentioned therefore it was rarely nurtured. It was not practiced in the home because self-love was never valued or respected as a sacred or personal act that needed to be practiced.

As I mentioned before, during my teen years and into adulthood, I struggled for many years with low self-esteem, low self-worth, no confidence, and body image issues. If you struggle with any of the same painful memories that I mentioned above these pillars will help you to heal and have more fulfilling personal and professional relationship.

Note to Self:

I will no longer allow the negative opinions of other people penetrate my mind or my heart. My life matters, I am a person of value, and I am more than enough.

My Secret Sauce Process

The ***Secret Sauce Process***, aka The ***Six Pillars of Love ThySELF***. These pillars will help you along your healing journey to love yourself, build your confidence, and maintain positive healthy balanced lifestyle. **The Six Pillars are self-love, personal boundaries, core values, personal standards, personal beliefs, and forgiveness**. Incorporating and maintaining these pillars into your life will ensure that your well-being is first and foremost your main concern. These six pillars are the game changers in my life and the reason why my life is unrecognizable today. I was a lost soul, before, during my marriage, and after my divorce. My life transformed and I began to see and love myself transparent, with all my flaws. Using these pillars and truly loving myself, I can honestly say, "I have taken back control of my life. I am able to maintain my triggers and I am not ashamed of my past challenges."

The Six Pillars of Love ThySELF

1. *Self-Love* is the greatest gift you can give to yourself: Loving yourself you create your own happiness, loving yourself you will take time to heal, loving yourself you will practice self-care, loving yourself will teach others to treat you with respect. When you love yourself, you are not comparing yourself to others. Loving yourself increases your self-esteem and self-worth. Loving yourself increases your self-confidence. Loving yourself is practicing self-care. Loving yourself will help you find your purpose. Loving your unique self brings freedom from toxic people and seeking the opinions and approval of others.

2. *Personal Boundaries* are vital to your personal development. Having boundaries is healthy. Having boundaries will show others how to love and respect you. Having boundaries will stop others from manipulating you for their benefit. Having

boundaries will give you the confidence to use your voice to say no instead of yes, all the time. Having boundaries will eliminate the toxic people in your life. Having boundaries will show you the true intentions of the people you allow in your life. Having boundaries keeps you in control of your emotions. Having boundaries will show your clients and co-workers how to treat you. Having boundaries keeps balance, peace, and positive energy in your life.

3. **Core Values** are vital to your personal growth. Core Values are your fundamental beliefs that have shaped and molded your ideas, opinions, and perceptions of what holds the most importance to you. Examples: *authenticity, honesty, accountability, dependable, loyal, faithfulness, commitment.*

4. **Personal Standards** are principles of beliefs, attitudes, and behaviors that are used to judge the quality and value of your life. Examples: *You don't want any drama in your life, You will not date a married man, You only date Christian men, Staying healthy and fit is important to you, Your will not date a mate that works a blue-collar job, You will be celibate until you get married.*

5. **Personal Beliefs** are what you believe to be true based on your opinions, attitude or perceptions regarding life, love, family, relationships, marriage, sex, and money. Examples: *Your belief in God, or your belief that there is more than one God, It is important to believe in yourself and your abilities, Marriage is sacred and is only between a man and women, Marriage is sacred and anyone can marry who they choose to marry regardless of their race or gender.*

6 **Forgiveness** is making a conscious effort to rid yourself of holding onto negative energy and emotional strongholds from being hurt by someone. Examples: *Forgive a person for hurting you, Forgive someone that lied on you, Forgive a person that verbally abused you, Forgive a person that stole something from you, Forgive a wayward child.*

As you create your pillars it may take some time for you to become consistent with them. It will also take time for your loved ones to become accustomed to the new you and the boundaries you have. You might have to do gentle reminders to your loved ones when they invade your boundaries. By the way, you do not have to contact your loved ones and inform them that you have these pillars that includes boundaries. It is your job to enforce these pillars in your life and insist that others respect them.

They will only do that when they see that you are consistently exercising them in your life. You might have other people in your life that are reluctant to abide by them. Be consistent. They will either comply with your new boundaries or stop begin a part of your circle. The people with good intentions will choose to stay in your life.

If you are struggling in any area of your life check to see which pillar has been compromised. Make the necessary adjustments to correct the unhealthy behaviors before they start to impact other areas of your life. To stop from being hurt emotionally from other, or manipulated, controlled or abused, your best defense is to learn how to love and appreciate who you are then you won't seek approval from your friends and family members. If you don't practice self-love and establish boundaries, you will continue to attract unhealthy people in your life and continue to have painful memories.

As I began to truly love myself, my self-esteem increased, my self-worth and self-confidence increase as well. I stopped body shamming myself and began to accept my body for the unique being that I am. Living by these principles I was able to heal from all the pain and guilt I held onto from past childhood memories, divorce, and abusive relationships. It is my hope that these six pillars will inspire, encourage and empower you on your healing journey to transform your life and become your ***Authentic Unique Self*** who is madly in love with yourself. I want this for you too.

I am cheering for your success on your healing journey.

Reflections

Dear Queen,

CONGRATULATIONS!! You have completed the entire journal. It is my hope that you have gained enough knowledge to help you establish a healing journey path. As you create your path, it is my hope that you will take the golden nuggets that you have acquired from this journal and apply them to your life.

As I have mentioned throughout the journal, the importance of self-love being vital to your personal growth. When you lack in this area, you open a gateway to unhealthy relationships, being taken advantage of by others, seeking approval from others, being bullied, and living a life that you aren't happy with. It is my desire that after reading this book you are ready to put the six pillars into action and take back control of your life. **You deserve it!**

Okay, my last suggestions for you are, first, please write down affirmations to say to yourself **every day**. Second, please hang the six pillars and the affirmations in high traffic areas in your place. The reason for this is to have them visible to you **every day** as you transform your life on your healing journey to **Authentic Self-Love** and becoming your **Authentic Unique Self.**

If you have a teen princess in your life and she would like her own journal, look for this title, **"Self-love: Your Healing Journal: The Soul of A Princess."** You can purchase this book on Amazon.

Take care and I wish you much success on your healing journey and becoming your **Authentic Unique Self.**

You are enough today, tomorrow, and forever more ... Love yourself. You are enough.

YOUR THOUGHTS

YOUR THOUGHTS

YOUR THOUGHTS

YOUR THOUGHTS

YOUR THOUGHTS

About the Author

Jacke L. Wilson is a mom of two beautiful adult daughters and a student of life. As a survivor of domestic abuse and an attempted suicide, these experiences have given her first-hand knowledge of the psychological and emotional damage abuse has on individuals and their families.

As an author of her first book, ***"Planning Your Escape …the KEY To Your Freedom"***, and the founder of R.I.T.E Connections & Recovery, LLC, in Arizona, she is living out her life purpose helping women to recover and rebuild their lives after being impacted by domestic and sexual abuse. As a Transformational Speaker, Life Recovery Coach, and Domestic and Sexual Violence Advocate, she uses her training and life experiences to inspire, motivate and empower women. It is her passion that drives her to help women to no longer feel defeated or defined by their past experiences from any form of trauma they have endured but to use that energy as fuel to heal and rebuild their lives.

Through her inspiring messages she shares her testimony of triumph, courage, and determination using varies platforms such as speaking engagements; TV and Radio Broadcast, weekly Social Media Webinars on Facebook, Instagram, Empowerment Group Sessions, Domestic and Sexual Violence Online Facebook Support Group, and a Women's Empowerment Book Club. Jacke is dedicated to inspiring and encouraging women, to move forward from feelings of guilt and shame becoming more confident and empowered, seeing themselves not only as a survivor but as a Champion.

Jacke understands the importance of healing and has spent several years researching healing and the effects it has on a person well-being. She has created a signature healing program that she uses in her practice as a life coach. She has written and self-published two books from her Self-Love Healing Book Series. First book titled, ***"Self-Love: The Soul of A Queen - Your Healing Journal"***, for women and the other book titled, ***"Self-Love: The Soul of A Princess - Your Healing Journal"***, for teenage girls. Both eBooks will be released May 30, 2020.

Email: jackewilsonspeaks@gmail.com
Facebook: https://www.facebook.com/authorjackelwilson
Instagram: https://www.instagram.com/jackelwilson
Amazon.com: https://www.amazon.com/author/jackewilson2019

Copyrighted

All rights reserved. This book or parts thereof may not be reproduced in any form, stored in any retrieval system, or transmitted in any form by any means – electronic, mechanical, including photocopying, recording, or otherwise - without prior written permission from the author or publisher, except as provided by United States of America copyright law.

This is a self-published book by author Jacalyn "Jacke" L. Wilson. Published and printed by Kindle Direct Publishing – Amazon.

ISBN- 9781071150245

ISBN-9781071150245

Printed in the United States of America.

All rights reserved. Any documentation listed in this book from other companies has been cited from the noted online websites and are indicated within the book.

                          Copyright © 2020 Jacke L. Wilson
                                All rights reserved.
                            ISBN-9781071150245
                            ISBN-9781071150245

Made in the USA
Columbia, SC
15 May 2022